THE ALPHABET OF GOD'S LOVE

26 REMINDERS OF GOD'S LOVING FAITHFULNESS TO HIS CHILDREN

J. JAY SANDERS

BARBOUR
PUBLISHING, INC.

The twenty-six letters of the alphabet are the basic building blocks of our English language. Without them, written communication would be impossible.

God's love is the foundational ingredient of our experience. Without it, our lives would be meaningless and empty.

Thankfully, God's love is unconditional and constant. It is directed toward us at all times—whether we realize it or not. And for those times when we forget, when we become caught up in the stresses and distractions of our world, this book can serve as a reminder of the powerful love God has for His children.

Just as the alphabet covers the entire breadth of our language, God's love covers the entire breadth of our daily lives. Read on to learn of God's love from A to Z. Find peace and encouragement in *The Alphabet of God's Love.*

I'm your Father, and I. . .

*A*ccept you as
My unique creation.

~

God created man in
His own image.
GENESIS 1:27

~

*We as Christians have
an image for
projection to the world.*

A. NAISMITH

I'm your Father, and I. . .

$\mathcal{B}$elieve you are precious and valuable.

~

The very hairs of your head
are all numbered.
So, do not fear;
you are more valuable
than many sparrows.
MATTHEW 10:30–31

I am the God of the stars.
Lift up thine eyes and see
As far as mortals may
Into eternity!
And stay thy heart on Me.

AMY CARMICHAEL

I'm your Father, and I. . .

*C*are about your hurts, tears, and all that touches you.

~

Casting all your anxiety on Him,
because He cares for you.
1 PETER 5:7

~

Worry says,
"God is a wimp."
Casting says,
"God is all powerful."

I'm your Father, and I. . .

$\mathcal{D}$esire only
what is best for you.

~

"For I know the plans that I have for you,"
declares the LORD,
"plans for welfare and not for calamity
to give you a future and a hope."
JEREMIAH 29:11

~

I will fling open wide a door of hope,
And I will give you back
Years that the locusts have devoured;
No good thing shall you lack.
NANCY HANSEN

I'm your Father, and I. . .

*E*stablish this promise.

~

The steps of a man are
established by the LORD,
And He delights in his way.
When he falls,
he will not be hurled headlong,
Because the LORD is
the One who holds his hand.
PSALM 37:23–24

~

No matter how
difficult the way
He promises to
hold us steady.

~

I'm your Father, and I. . .

*F*orgive all your sins,
even future ones
yet uncommitted.

~

"Behold,
the Lamb of God who
takes away the sin of the world!"
JOHN 1:29

~

The cross crosses out

ALL my sin.

I'm your Father, and I. . .

*G*ive the Holy Spirit to
assist you with your prayers.

~

In the same way
the Spirit also helps our weakness;
for we do not know
how to pray as we should,
but the Spirit Himself intercedes for us
with groanings too deep for words.
ROMANS 8:26

~

*When we pray
it is as a duet,
not a solo.*

13

I'm your Father, and I. . .

*H*ave no intentions
of leaving or
rejecting you.

~

"I will be with you;
I will not fail you or forsake you."
JOSHUA 1:5

And none shall pluck us
from that hand.
Eternally we are secure.
Though heaven and earth
shall pass away,
His word forever shall endure.

MRS. M. E. RAE

I'm your Father, and I. . .

*I*nvite you to let Me into your heart.

~

"Behold, I stand at the door and knock;
if anyone hears My voice and opens the door,
I will come in to him and will dine with him,
and he with Me."
REVELATION 3:20

~

This place is occupied.
DR. F. W. BOREHAM

I'm your Father, and I. . .

*J*ust want you to know that I love you.

~

"The LORD your God is in your midst,
A victorious warrior.
He will exult over you with joy,
He will be quiet in His love,
He will rejoice over you with shouts of joy."
ZEPHANIAH 3:17

~

Love bore our sins away;
Love gave us life anew;
Love opened wide the gates of heaven;
Love gave us work to do.

RUTH A. ATWELL

I'm your Father, and I. . .

*K*eep a protective eye
on you.

~

For he who touches you,
touches the apple of His eye.
ZECHARIAH 2:8

~

Jehovah-Sabaoth

encamps around

His children.

~

I'm your Father, and I. . .

*L*ove you.
One can never say
those words enough.

~

Walk in love,
just as Christ also loved you
and gave Himself up for us.
EPHESIANS 5:2

~

Lord, help me over life's rough road
To share my brother's heavy load.
Since Christ bore mine for me.
S. E. BURROW

I'm your Father, and I. . .

Marvel at how you
have grown and changed.

~

Grow in the grace and knowledge
of our Lord and Savior Jesus Christ.
2 PETER 3:18

~

Though I am not what I ought to be,
nor what I wish to be,
nor yet hope to be, I can
truly say I am not what I once was,
a slave to sin and Satan.

JOHN NEWTON

I'm your Father, and I. . .

$\mathcal{N}$ever ignore your Advocate.

~

My little children,
I am writing these things to you
so that you may not sin.
And if anyone sins,
we have an Advocate with the Father,
Jesus Christ the righteous.
1 JOHN 2:1

Christ's work as Advocate comes
into operation as soon as we sin. . . .
We have a lovely word in Africa
used to express this idea.
An advocate or comforter is
sometimes called a
"kasendo mukwashi."
The first word, "kasendo," means
"a blood brother,"
one with whom a solemn covenant
sealed in blood has been made.
The second word, "mukwashi," means
"one who helps by laying hold."
The Lord is both to us.

T. ERNEST WILSON

I'm your Father, and I. . .

*O*ffered My son so
that we could be
together forever.

~

For God so loved the world,
that He gave His only begotten Son,
that whoever believes in Him
shall not perish,
but have eternal life.
JOHN 3:16

~

Enough said.

24

With God all things are possibl
Matthew 19:26

I'm your Father, and I. . .

$\mathcal{P}$raise your achievements both small and great.

~

Let another praise you,
and not your own mouth.
PROVERBS 27:2

~

Surpassing all other honors

is the King's,

"Well done!"

DR. NORTHCOTE DECK

I'm your Father, and I. . .

Quickly run to your aid
anytime, anywhere.

~

For you were continually straying like sheep,
but now you have returned to
the Shepherd and Guardian of your souls.
1 PETER 2:25

*In the town of Woeden in Germany,
on the tower of a fine church building
is the carved figure of a lamb.
It was placed there to
commemorate the remarkable escape
from death of a workman who fell
from the high scaffolding when
the tower was being built.
At the moment of his fall a flock of
sheep was being driven by,
and he had fallen on one of the lambs,
which was crushed to death.
The carved figure of the lamb
was placed there to commemorate the
incident, and also to remind all
who came that way of the Lamb
of God who died to save sinners.*

A. NAISMITH

27

I'm your Father, and I. . .

*Rejoice over
our friendship.*

~

Greater love
has no one than this,
that one lay down his life
for his friends.
JOHN 15:13

What a friend we have in Jesus,
All our sins and griefs to bear.
What a privilege to carry
Everything to God in prayer.

JOSEPH SCRIVEN

I'm your Father, and I. . .

*S*ee every moment
of your life.

~

O LORD,
You have searched me and known me.
You know when I sit down
and when I rise up;
You understand my thought from afar.
You scrutinize my path and my lying down,
And are intimately acquainted
with all my ways.
Even before there is a word on my tongue,
Behold, O LORD, You know it all.
PSALM 139: 1–4

We're in His hand,
that mighty Hand
That flung a universe in space,
That guides the sun
and the moon and stars
And holds the planets
in their place.

MRS. M. E. RAE

THE ALPHABET OF GOD'S LOVE

I'm your Father, and I. . .

*T*ell you that
My eyes search for you.

~

For the eyes of the LORD move
to and fro throughout the earth
that He may strongly support
those whose heart is completely His.
2 CHRONICLES 16:9

~

*He intently looks for
those intent on being
totally surrendered to
His Lordship.*

I'm your Father, and I. . .

$\mathcal{U}$nderstand
your weaknesses.

~

For we do not have a high priest who cannot
sympathize with our weaknesses,
but One who has been tempted
in all things as we are,
yet without sin.
HEBREWS 4:15

~

Jesus loves me this I know,
For the Bible tells me so.
Little ones to Him belong—
They are weak but He is strong.
WILLIAM BRADBURY

THE ALPHABET OF GOD'S LOVE

I'm your Father, and I. . .

$\mathcal{V}$alue you.

~

So, do not fear;
you are more valuable
than many sparrows.
MATTHEW 10:31

~

*Nobody knows
what a human is worth.
How do you put
a price tag on the cross?*

~

I'm your Father, and I. . .

*W*alk you through the dark times.

~

Even though I walk through
the valley of the shadow of death,
I fear no evil,
for You are with me.
PSALM 23:4

~

Confidence—
"I will fear no evil."

H. A. IRONSIDE

I'm your Father, and I give you. . .

χ(Christos),
anointing your life with My power.

~

You prepare a table before me
in the presence of my enemies;
You have anointed
my head with oil.
PSALM 23:5

~

*Anointed sheep
do not fear an unanointed enemy.*

I'm your Father, and I. . .

*Y*earn to have fellowship with you.

~

What we have seen and heard
we proclaim to you also,
so that you too may have
fellowship with us;
and indeed our fellowship is
with the Father,
and with His Son Jesus Christ.
1 JOHN 1:3

To walk with God—
'tis not too late to join
That holy band
who soared above the sod
Of transient things,
of weights, besetting sins,
And feel the mighty pulse
of life with God.

JBN

I'm your Father, and I. . .

*Z*ealously look to the day that you come home to be with Me.

~

"If I go and prepare a place for you,
I will come again and receive you to Myself,
that where I am, there you may be also."
JOHN 14:3

~

*"To Christians heaven is
their everlasting home.
The most marvelous thing about it is
that God has prepared it
for those who love Him."*

MATTHEW HENRY